Now I Know

Go to Sleep

by MELVIN AND GILDA BERGER

SCHOLASTIC INC.

New York Toronto London Auckland Sydney
Mexico City New Delhi Hong Kong Buenos Aires

ISBN 10: 0-439-02450-1
ISBN 13: 978-0-439-02450-1

12 11 10 9 8 7 6 5 4 3 2 1   7 8 9 10 11 12/0

Printed in the U.S.A.
First Printing, September 2007
Book design by Nancy Sabato

Everyone needs sleep.

Your brain works all day.

ZOOM!

ZOOM!

Your muscles work all day.

6

Your brain gets tired.

Your muscles get tired, too.

The day is over.

It's time to go to bed.

Do you read before
you go to sleep?

Or do you listen to a story?

Do you listen to music?

Or do you cuddle with a toy?

While you sleep —

—your muscles rest.
—your heart
   slows down.
—your body mends.
—you grow.
—you dream.
—and your brain
   is hard at work.

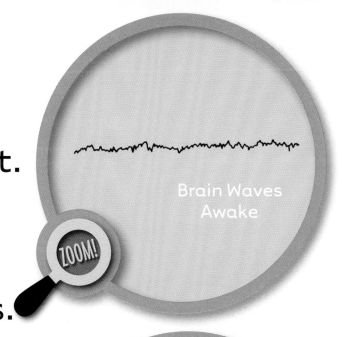

Brain Waves
Awake

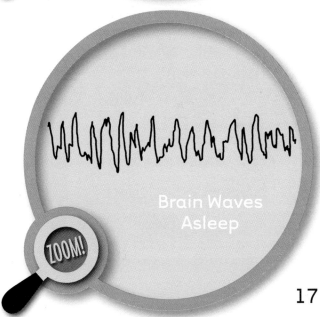

Brain Waves
Asleep

DID YOU KNOW?

Most children need about ten hours of sleep a night.

How long do *you* sleep?

How do you wake up?

Sleep ten hours —
and you wake up happy.

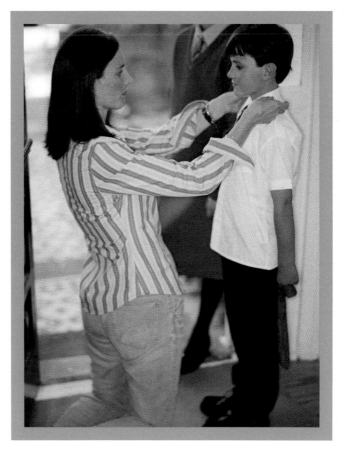

Sleep ten hours — and you're ready to start the day.

Too little sleep — and you wake up tired.

Too little sleep — and you're sleepy all day.

Too little sleep — and you're grumpy all day.

Oops! You may also have more accidents.

Snuggle in!

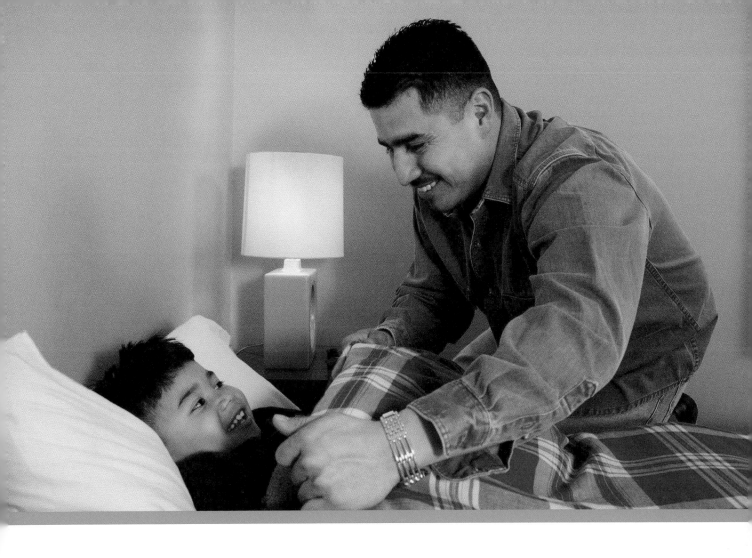

Everyone needs to sleep.

Some sleep in funny places.

Some sleep in funny positions.

But at night we all sleep in beds.

ZZZZZ!
Sweet dreams!

GLOSSARY

Brain: The organ inside your head that controls the body and helps you think and have feelings.

Brain waves: Little waves of electricity that your brain gives off all the time.

Heart: The organ that pumps blood through your body.

Heart beats: The pumping movements of the heart.

Muscles: The parts of your body that help you move.